CTC : Campus To Corporate

The Unvarnished Truth

Sanjeev Chaubey

BookLeaf Publishing

India | USA | UK

Made with ❤ on the BookLeaf Publishing Platform
www.bookleafpub.in
www.bookleafpub.com

Dedication

To the ***ambitious college graduates and future leaders***, who will shape the world with their ideas, passion, and courage. I believe that this book will be your guiding light as you navigate the exciting yet challenging journey from ***CAMPUS To CORPORATE***

I dedicate this book to your success, growth, and unwavering pursuit of excellence. With love and best wishes, may this book inspire, guide, and motivate you to ***become the best version of yourself*** and unlock your full potential.

I also dedicate this book to the unsung heroes - the ***Career Counselors, Mentors, and Guides*** who selflessly devote their time and expertise to shape the careers of countless Young Minds. Your tireless efforts, wisdom, and generosity have inspired me to write this book, and I hope it honors your contributions to the lives of others.

To the leaders of today, who are shaping the corporate world, I offer this reminder: The Young Minds we empower today will become the leaders of tomorrow. Let us inspire, guide, and nurture them, that they may build on our legacy and create a brighter future for all.

Preface

CTC : CAMPUS TO CORPORATE

Welcome to **CAMPUS To CORPORATE (CTC)**, your guide to navigating the exciting yet challenging journey from academic life to the corporate world. As someone who has experienced the ups and downs of this transition, I was motivated to write this book to help students and young professionals *avoid the pitfalls and seize the opportunities.*

With over **two decades of corporate experience**, I've had the privilege of interviewing thousands of candidates and witnessing firsthand the challenges they face during their transition from campus to corporate life. I've seen the struggles, the setbacks, and the successes. And I've learned that *the first 21 days are crucial* in setting the tone for a successful career.

The purpose of CTC is to provide *practical advice, real-life examples, and actionable strategies* to help you succeed in your career. This book is designed for college students, recent graduates, and young professionals who are looking to make a smooth transition into the corporate world.

Throughout the book, we'll explore topics such as building a strong foundation for your career, developing essential skills for corporate success, navigating office politics, and creating a personal brand. This journey is designed to be a self ***transformative 21-day experience***, with each of the 21 chapters offering practical advice and actionable tips to help you develop the habits, mindset, and skills necessary to succeed in the corporate world.

As you read through this book, I encourage you to engage with the material, reflect on your own strengths and weaknesses, and apply the learnings to your own career journey. Remember, your career is a marathon, not a sprint. Be receptive, stay committed, and ***you'll be amazed at the positive changes you'll experience!***

Acknowledgements

I would like to express my heartfelt gratitude to the numerous individuals who have contributed to the creation of this book.

First and foremost, I thank my readers, who have been a constant source of encouragement and motivation. Your emails, messages, and comments on social media platforms like **Insta, Facebook, LinkedIn, YouTube,** and others have meant the world to me.

I am also deeply indebted to *my corporate colleagues, past and present, who have shared their knowledge, experiences, and insights* with me over the years. Many of you may not even realize how your contributions have shaped this book, but I am grateful for the invaluable lessons I've learned from you.

To the many corporate aspirants I've met in colleges, forums, and other platforms, I thank you for sharing your concerns, aspirations, and dreams with me. Your voices have been instrumental in shaping the content of this book, and I hope it will serve as a valuable resource for you as you navigate your own career journeys.

Thank you all for being part of this journey.

Lastly, I would like to extend my sincere thanks and appreciation to **_BookLeaf Publishing Company_** for giving me the opportunity to share my thoughts and experiences with the world. Your support and guidance have been invaluable, and I look forward to future collaborations!

1. CRACK THE CODE : MOP2 Formula Remains Same for all !

The day arrives, with nervous delight
Campus interviews, a make-or-break sight
Selectors from MNCs, with eyes so keen
Students excited, yet struggling to be seen

They know their subjects, but struggle to express
Lacking confidence, in their own success
Some falter on communication, others on company facts
Unprepared, they face the selection panel's acts

But here's a secret, to crack the code
MOP², a formula to abode
Market, Organization, Product, and People too
Learn about them, and your confidence will shine through

Research the market, trends and demands
Know the company's mission, values, and plans
Familiarize yourself with their products and services

And **_learn about the people,_** who'll be interviewing you
with expertise

With **MOP^2, you'll be well-prepared**
To face the selectors, with confidence unscarred
So don't be nervous, don't be shy
Use MOP^2, and watch your dreams fly high

To all the young students, with aspirations bright
Remember MOP^2, and shine with all your light!

2. DARE TO DREAM

Come out of Comfort Zone!

With dreams in their eyes, and fire in their soul,
They step out of college, into the corporate role.
Their minds are ablaze, with passion and desire,
To make a mark, to leave a burning fire.

They seek the perfect job, with challenges and thrill,
A role that ignites their spark, and lets their talent fulfill.
They envision a workspace, where creativity flows free,
Where innovation meets passion, and success is the decree.

But reality checks in, with a harsh, cruel tone,
As they face the grind, and the corporate throne.
The job they land, may not be their dream come true,
But they must adapt, and make the best of what they can do.

They learn to navigate, the office politics and games,
To balance work and life, and manage stress and flames.
They discover their strengths, and work on their weaknesses too,
And slowly but surely, they start to make their mark anew.

Though the journey's tough, and the road ahead is unclear,
They persevere and push on, through laughter and through tears.
For they know that success, is not just a destination,
But a journey of growth, of learning, and of education.

So here's to the young ones, who dare to dream and roam,
Who leave the comfort of campus, to take on the corporate home.
May their passions ignite, and their talents shine so bright,
And may they find success, in the dark of night.

3. EEE - Education | Environment | Experience What's in Your Control, work on that !

They sit in the auditorium, with eyes wide with cheer
The induction program, a new journey to clear
Boys and girls, with dreams in their hearts
Ready to take on the world, and play their parts

But as they listen to policies, and rules of the game
They realize that textbooks, didn't prepare them for this claim
Theories and concepts, that once seemed so bright
Now seem distant, as they face the corporate light

So, here's a piece of advice, as they start this new ride
What you learned in school, was just a typical guide
Now it's time to learn, through the Environment and Experience
To adapt, to evolve, and to make your own presence

Don't be disappointed, if theories don't apply
For the real world is different, and you must ask why

Observe, listen, and learn, from those around
And soon you'll find your footing, on this corporate
ground

So welcome to the real world, where learning never
stops
Where experiences shape you, and your growth never
drops
Enjoy this new journey, with an open heart and mind
And you'll find success, in this corporate grind.

4. ROLE : STEER TO VOLUNTEER

Find your Own Tribe !

They gathered in the conference room, eager and bright
Assigned to roles, without a choice in sight
Some to sales, some to marketing, tech support, and
more
Like school kids sectioned off, without a say in store

No one asked what they loved, what sparked their fire
Just a random assignment, without heart's desire
They remembered school days, when sections were
assigned
But this felt different, with careers on the line

They made friends in their sections, shared laughs and
stories too
But now they're apart, with no time to break through
No watercooler chats, no snack breaks to share
Just solitary workstations, with tea/coffee to prepare

But here's a secret, to thriving in this space
Networking is key, to finding your corporate pace
Attend office events, join groups that align

Volunteer for projects, that spark your shine

Make friends with colleagues, from different
departments too
Share your stories, and learn from theirs, it's true
In this corporate jungle, it's easy to feel alone
But with a network of friends, you'll find your way back
home

So don't be discouraged, by your assigned role
Find ways to connect, and make your corporate soul
Networking is power, to breaking down walls
And finding friends in the corporate halls.

5. POOCHNE ME KYA JAATA HAI (Nothing Wrong in Asking)

They stepped into their office, with hearts so bright
Expecting a warm welcome, a guiding light
Like their first day of school, with hands held tight
But here, the HR team, was busy in sight

Hardworking and Resourceful, but with no time to spare
They handed them over, to their functional leaders with care
The leaders spoke at length, with words so bold
But the new trainees listened, with minds that grew cold

Their minds were overwhelmed, like a computer with too much data
Only 100Kb of info, stuck in their mental stata
They felt lost and alone, like navigators without a map
Uncertain of their destination, with a future that looked flat

But here's a piece of advice, to help them find their way
Navigate like explorers, through the corporate day
Don't hesitate to ask, to seek and to explore

For clarity is key, to unlocking the corporate door

As Steve Jobs once said: "Those who don't ask, don't get."

So, ask, seek, and explore, and you'll find your way
Through the corporate jungle, to a brighter day.

6. IT'S OFFICE PERIOD
No Break Allowed !

She walks through the glass door, with confidence high
A new face in the corporate sky
But soon she's lost in a sea of men
Her voice unheard, her thoughts unseen again

She struggles to cope, with the workload and stress
Her periods arrive, but no rest
No leaves, no relaxation, just a sympathetic ear
But who thinks of her pain, her tears, her fear?

Everyone's kind to their wives and daughters dear
But the girl in the office, is someone's daughter too, isn't clear?
She's a woman, a warrior, with a heart that beats strong
She deserves respect, empathy, and a helping hand all
day long

So, here's to the women, who brave the corporate grind
May your strength and resilience, forever be on your
mind

Keep pushing forward, don't let the struggles bring you down
You are powerful, capable, and worthy of every crown.

7. DESKSIDE CHAT

Don't make it Beachside!

They sit at their desks, amidst colleagues so fine
Experienced and wise, with stories to divine
Chit-chat begins, and they share with glee
Their journeys, their struggles, and their destiny

But amidst the laughter, and the friendly tone
Lies a hidden truth, that's not always shown
They speak of godfathers, and corporate might
Of worshiping the lords, who hold the power tight

But beware, young one, of such gossip and sway
Stay focused on work, and drive the distractions away
Seek out those who speak, of process and productivity
too
They'll help you tackle tasks, and see your goals anew

Connect with like-minded souls, who share your vision
and fire
People connect with their kind, it's a corporate desire
Find your tribe, your allies, who'll help you grow and

thrive
And navigate the corporate world, with a sense of
purpose alive

So listen and learn, but don't get swayed
Stay true to your goals, and keep your focus displayed
It's who you know, that matters, but also what you do
Stay connected, stay focused, and your
dreams will come true.

8. CLUTTER TO CLEAR

Goals are Mine!

The mail arrives, with goals that flash so bright
Roles defined, and expectations in sight
They feel smart, capable, and ready to take flight
But as they read on, doubts begin to ignite

The goals seem unrealistic, a heavy load to bear
They wonder if they're achievable, or just a distant care
To accept or negotiate, that's the question at hand
But the mail says clearly, "Goals are non-negotiable, stand"

The package was negotiable, but goals are set in stone
They're left with a dilemma, and a decision to call home
But here's a piece of advice, before you make your move
Go back and talk to your manager, and seek to improve

Remember MOP Square, and ask your manager to share
The aspects that led to these goals, and show you care
Seek information, and clarification, to be sure and bright
That your goals are realistic, and achievable in sight

And when you're clear on your goals, and your path is
defined
You'll soar to new heights, with confidence aligned
Your goals will be achievable, and your success will
shine
By seeking clarity, you'll make your goals truly mine.

9. NEED MAP to NAVIGATE

"My Action Plan"

Goals are set, and now it's time to begin
To navigate the journey, and reach the destination within
A map is needed, to chart the course ahead
But here, the map is different, it's one that's carefully spread

It's not a physical map, but a plan of action so fine
A roadmap to success, that's tailored to your design
It's called "My Action Plan", a MAP to guide your way
To ensure you reach your goals, come what may

As you're SMART, your roadmap should be too
With Specific actions, Measurable steps to pursue
Achievable tasks, that are Realistic and true
And Time allocated to each, to see your goals shine through

So create your MAP, with precision and care
Break down your goals, into smaller steps to share
Make it SMART, and make it yours, a plan that's unique
And you'll be on your way, to achieving your goals
unique

With your MAP in hand, you'll navigate with ease
And reach your destination, with success and expertise
So don't delay, create your MAP today
And start your journey, to achieving your goals in a
SMART way!

By following your MAP, you'll stay on track
And make progress towards, your goals, no looking back
You'll build momentum, and gain confidence too
And achieving your goals, will become a reality anew

10. SWITCH on GPRS
Your Roadside Assistance !

In the corporate world, you're ready to roll
With goals set high, and a heart that's whole
But navigation's key, to reach your desired place
That's where GPRS comes in, with a smile on its face

G - Gear up, with the right tools in hand
To tackle challenges, and make your goals stand
P - Prepare for the unforeseen, with a flexible mind
For speed breaks and terrains, that will test your grind

R - Reflect back, on your journey so far
See where you started, and how much you've travelled in
your car
Gain confidence and clarity, by looking back in time
And you'll be ready to move forward, with a renewed
rhyme

S - Strategize, with a plan that's new
What worked for you, and what didn't, it's time to break
through

Define what will work further, and make adjustments
with care
And you'll be navigating smoothly, with GPRS guiding
you there

Just like a driver, with GPRS by their side
Reaches their destination, with a confident stride
***You'll navigate the corporate world, with ease and with
flair***
And reach your goals, without a single care

With every turn, and every twist
GPRS will guide you, and help you persist
Through the ups and downs, of the corporate ride
You'll stay on track, with GPRS as your guide

With GPRS by your side, you'll conquer any terrain
***Achieve your goals, and reach new heights of success
and gain***
remember GPRS, and its navigational might
And you'll be unstoppable, shining with delight!

11. FAC to VIVA

Field Accompaniment Call

Remember field trips, fun and carefree days?
In school and college, we'd explore in joyful ways
But in the corporate world, it's a different tale
FAC, or Field Accompaniment Call, can be a painful gale

No welcoming guides, no explanations so fine
Just harsh words, like "F*** off", a far cry from a picnic's shine
The young minds were shocked, their experience a test
But here's a lesson learned, to help them do their best

Treat field calls as practical classes, not a picnic spree
Observe, try, and learn, just like mixing chemicals with glee
Note the behaviors, of seniors and market folk too
Try your own approach, and see what works, and what to pursue

Experiment, take risks, and don't be afraid to fail
For in the process, you'll discover, and your skills will set

sail
So don't go blank, or bare-handed, be prepared to face
The challenges of the market, and the corporate pace

Advice to the young minds:

Don't be discouraged by harsh words, or a bad experience
Instead, learn from it, and use it as a stepping stone to
excellence
Treat field calls as opportunities, to grow and to learn
And remember, experimentation, is the key to success
that yearns.

12. SITE to SIGHT

Love at 1st SITE !

It was a field call, a chance encounter so fine
Hearts collided, souls aligned, in a corporate shrine
A site of safety, yet control was lost that day
An accident of love, that changed life's way

Advice was given, to stay away from attractive sights
Lest damage be done, and hearts take flight
But warnings were ignored, and hearts drew near
***A gentle touch, a question whispered, "Are you the one I
hold dear?"***

It wasn't a college crush, but a corporate spark
A connection so strong, it left its mark
Conversations flowed, of aspirations and dreams
A bond was formed, in the corporate scheme

Questions were asked, of identity and might
"Who are you today, and what do you aspire to ignite?"
"Do you believe, or think, when decisions draw near?"
"Are you still tied to family strings, or do you hold your

own gear?"

If you're a young mind, with a heart so bright
Focus on your work, for the first three years, day and
night
Then, if love happens, check your eligibility with care
**Take a six-month probation, on the love track, and seek
confirmation to share**

Love can happen anywhere, college to corporate, it's true
**But remember to balance, your heart and your career,
anew.**

13. Take Off to Bu** Off !
The Deployment Debacle

Young minds soaring high and bright,
Eager for deployment, day and night.
Cross-city travels, market dynamics too,
Challenges awaited, with lessons anew.

The assembly hall, a familiar sight,
White screen glowing, projector shining bright.
"SOAR HIGH!" the title slide did say,
Hearts racing fast, excitement on its way.

The hardworking team, with lists in hand,
Deploying platoons, across the land.
North to South, East to West, the routes did unfold,
Faces lit up, like semester results to behold.

Chit-chat and laughter, filled the air,
Who's going where? What to pack? With care.
Airlines' limits, luggage weights did abound,
Excitement building, like campus selection all around.

But then, the next slide, a title so fine,
"Travel Arrangements" - hearts did align.
Only to find, 3rd AC, Chair Car, or Volvo too,
The young minds' faces, fell, with dreams anew.

Faced down, excitement waned, they walked away,
A lesson learned, in the corporate way.
Company coffers drained, yet Director soar with ease,
In Business Class Comfort, while others feel the squeeze.

Marketing spends, on unknown ads galore,
Incentives withheld, from achievers evermore.
A culture to adapt, morale to keep high,
Soar on dreams' wings, and touch the open sky.

For someday, they'll fly Business Class too,
Their hard work paying off, with success shining
through.
Keep dreams alive, and never give up the quest,
Soar high, young minds, and let your spirits find rest.

14. Four Not Seven !
Chandni Chowk to China

In a six-day week grind, young minds astray,
Wondering why India's pace is slow today.
While Japan and China switch to four days' rest,
New India demands seven days of endless test.

Confused and worn, they question the way,
"Work hard, work hard," yet soft skills hold the sway.
In college, they learned to win with a gentle touch,
But now, hard work is touted, leaving them in a hunch.

Hard things break first, soft things bend and thrive,
Young minds are torn, unsure of how to survive.
Unlearn and learn, the functional head did say,
But which path to follow, they're lost, come what may.

Advice to young minds, stay calm and serene,
Look within, find your fit, and make it a dream.
If it's not fun, fall in love with the task,
Recall college days, and let passion embark.

If it doesn't work, it's time to reassess,
Maybe you're in the wrong place, it's time to confess.
Bunk the class, join another, find your heart's desire,
Don't settle for less, young minds, your spirit on fire.

So stay true to yourself, don't lose your way,
In the chaos of work life, seize the day.
Remember, soft skills matter, and hard work's not the test,
Find your passion, and success will find its nest.

15. Perplexing to Presenting Leave Your Mark in Dark !

Two weeks have passed, young minds take the stage,
Presenting learnings, in a corporate age.
Different functions, cities, and markets explored,
But will their findings impress, or leave them poor?

Experienced eyes watch, with critical gaze,
Will they ask tough questions, or offer praise?
Unlike college exams, where cramming's the test,
Here, progress reports matter, and expectations are best.

Slides are prepared, with AI's guiding hand,
But clarity of thought is what truly makes a stand.
Articulation matters, but ideas must be bright,
AI can't generate thoughts, that shine with human light.

A young mind presents, on brand image and share,
But the CEO asks, "How will you show us you care?"
Not just data and facts, but a plan to take the lead,
Increase brand value, and market share to proceed.

Another presents, on product portfolios so fine,
But misses the mark, on what actions to design.
Should products be added, or cut to make it lean?

The CEO seeks answers, to make the business serene.

Advice to young minds, when presenting your case,
*Share market understanding, with a clear call to action's
pace.*
Show how your findings, can take the company to new
heights,
Ask for support needed, to make your vision take flight.

Don't just present data, present a plan to thrive,
Show how your ideas, can help the company stay alive.
Remember, young minds, your presentation is key,
To unlock opportunities, and make your mark with glee.

*So, young minds, when you present, think of a PPF
account too,*
Reflect on the company's PAST, its achievements shining
through.
Show the PRESENT scenario, challenges, and
competition so bright,
And shape the FUTURE with your ideas, a vision that's
clear and in sight.

16. Ready To Roar?
Ye Dil Maange More !

Young minds empowered, with vision in sight,
Ready to roar, with a goal to ignite.
Leadership guidance, has fueled their desire,
To achieve and succeed, with a burning fire.

Expectations high, like flying in the sky,
Even if they fall, they'll still touch the high.
College days recalled, with memories so bright,
AIR #3 was the aim, but 300 was still alright.

But corporate life's different, with targets to meet,
100% is satisfactory, not exceptional to greet.
Young minds must adapt, to this new pace,
And strive to achieve, with a smile on their face.

Advice to young minds, as you start your quest,
Ask for quarterly goals, and reviews to assess your best.
Check if you're on track, or slipping away,
Seek help if needed, to seize the day.

Under commit, over deliver, in your early days,
Learn the market dynamics, and find your ways.
Then switch to over commit, over deliver with flair,

And show the world your strength, with a confident air.

To team leaders, a word of caution, we say,
Don't set goals too high, that lead to dismay.
Give small goals, help them achieve, and encourage to soar,
Like athletes in training, who start with a 10-meter score.

Guide them, support them, and watch them grow,
From young minds to leaders, with a story to show.
Remember, leadership is not just about setting goals high,
But also about helping others, reach for the sky.

17. Break The Rules Made by Fools !

Young minds sailing, in the corporate sea,
Need a coach to guide, and set them free.
Three lessons learned, to achieve and thrive,
Break the rules, but ethically, stay alive.

Doing the same, yields the same result,
To achieve differently, a new path to construct.
Rules are made, by those of the past,
But now it's your era, and you know what will last.

Take Galileo Galilei, who dared to defy,
The geocentric model, and reached for the sky.
He broke the rules, of Aristotle's view,
And proved the Earth revolves, around the Sun anew.

Or think of Steve Jobs, who merged art and tech,
And broke the rules, of what a phone should connect.
He revolutionized, the way we communicate,
And created a new norm, that changed the world's fate.

Nike and Jordan, a story to tell,
Breaking the rule, of the red color to sell.
Penalized, yet victorious, in the end,

A brand image built, that will forever transcend.

A line of caution, to remember and heed,
Don't break the ethics, that your soul and heart need.
But rules that hinder, and don't let you grow,
Break them, and make way, for a new path to show.

In this corporate war, where wins are key,
Set your own trend, and make history.
The next gen will come, with knowledge and might,
But for now, it's your turn, to shine with all your light.

18. Mistakes were Made But Not by Me !

Young minds observe, as seniors take the stage,
Mistakes are made, but denied, and blame is engaged.
They watch as others, escape with ease and guile,
And wonder, should they follow, this questionable style.

But when in doubt, they reach out to their guide,
Their coach, who helps them navigate, with a gentle stride.
He shows them two paths, with different outcomes clear,
And helps them understand, which one to hold dear.

If they make a mistake, and don't admit, they'll find
A path that's downward: A - B - C - D - E
A - Avoidance
B - Blame
C - Chalta Hai
D - Dip in their career
E - End of their growth.

But if they own up, and admit, they'll see
A different outcome: A - B - C - D - E
A - Acceptance
B - Beginning to analyze

C - Change in their approach
D - Driving themselves to improve,
E - Excellence, the ultimate goal they'll achieve.

With clarity and confidence, they choose the right way,
Thanks to their coach, who showed them the light of
day.
Young minds decide, to take the high road, and own,
Their mistakes, and learn, and grow, and make
their spirit known.

***Remember, it's better to be alone than being in a wrong
company,***
A truth that's learned, as they navigate the corporate sea.
For average performers, it's the standard, the norm,
But for young minds, excellence is the goal to form.

So be careful while choosing your tribe,
***For the company you keep, will shape your corporate
jive.***
Seek out those who inspire, who motivate and who
guide,
And together, you'll soar, to heights you never
thought you'd glide.

19. Beyond the Flock !
Unleash Your Potential

Young minds in corporate, need guidance on their way,
A coach to companion, through each new day.
But coaches know, their time is limited and rare,
"You need to find your tribe," they advise with care.

"Find those with integrity, values, and heart,
Who innovate, push boundaries, and play their part."
But beware, dear young minds, of the company you keep,
Lest you forget your true self, and your spirit sleep.

A story's shared, of an eagle's might,
Who laid an egg, in a chick farm's sight.
The eaglet grew, among the chicks' crew,
And learned to waddle, with feet that weren't true.

It never flew, though it had the wings,
For the chicks around, said, "We don't do things."
One day, it saw, an eagle soaring high,
And wished to join, but the chicks said, "You can't try."

The moral's clear, don't become what you're not,
Find your true self, and your potential will be caught.

Don't let others define, who you're meant to be,
Explore, discover, and soar, wild and free.

In the corporate world, where growth is key,
Remember, you're an eagle, meant to fly high and free.
Don't waddle with the chicks, when you can soar with
pride,
Find your true self, and your potential will be your
guide.

As the saying goes, if you associate with eagles, you'll
know,
How to soar to great heights, and make your spirit glow.
A single conversation with the right person can be more
valuable,
Than years of study, or lessons that are theoretical.

So seek out mentors, who can guide you on your way,
And surround yourself with people, who inspire you
each day.
For the company you keep, will shape your destiny,
And help you unlock your potential, in harmony.

20. Call of Action

In corporate's maze, where growth is key,
Seek clarity within, to unlock destiny.
Ask yourself the questions, that spark the mind,
And answer genuinely, to leave the doubts behind.

1. What's the one bold decision I'd make, if I knew I'd succeed?
2. Am I running towards my dreams, or fleeing from my fears?
3. What's the attitude I wear, that fuels my fire or dims my spark?
4. If everyone in the company mirrored my work ethic, would we achieve growth?
5. What's the one self-sabotaging habit I can break free from?
6. What's the innovative idea brewing within me, waiting to disrupt?
7. Am I using my time like a precious gem, or letting it slip away?
8. What's the good habit I've neglected, that I can revive to boost growth?
9. How do I consistently earn the respect of my peers and mentors?
10. What would a creative genius do in my shoes, to

solve challenges?

11. What's the internal spark that fuels my growth, and external trigger?

12. What is my USP, which makes me invaluable?

13. What's the selfless act I can do, that will ignite purpose and fulfillment?

14. What's the one thing that makes me proud to be me, and how can I leverage?

15. Am I paralyzed by fear of failure, or emboldened by the thrill?

16. What's the impossible task I'll tackle next, to push limits?

17. What are the daily habits I'm building, that will shape destiny?

18. How much have I grown, and what lessons have I learned?

19. What's the lasting legacy I want to leave, when my journey comes full circle?

20. What's the one question I'm afraid to ask, that could change everything?

21. What's the first step I'll take today, to move closer to my dreams?

Answer these questions, and you'll find your way,
To knowing yourself, and seizing the corporate day.
For success is not a destination, but a journey to embark,
And knowing yourself is the key, to leave your mark.

21. CTC - Cost to Cut !

Young minds in corporate, 21 days have passed,
Transition phase over, they've learned so much at last.
The culture shock fades, as they start to feel at home,
Adopting the corporate way, they're no longer alone.

Excitement builds, as new financial year begins,
Appraisal letters shared, with revised CTCs that spin.
Seniors' reactions mixed, as new numbers are revealed,
Young minds watch eagerly, as their seniors' fortunes are
sealed.

Like students awaiting grades, they watch with bated
breath,
*Their turn will come soon, but for now, they eagerly gaze
at their seniors' wealth.*
They see the highs and lows, the smiles and the frowns,
As their seniors react, to their revised CTCs, with mixed
emotions that abound.

But shock sets in, as grading systems are revealed,
A new reality unfolds, their expectations unsealed.
College CGPA, a distant memory now,
Cumulative Grade Point Average, a different vow.

Corporate CGPA, a new beast to tame,
Common Goal Performance Appraisal, a different game.
Coach steps in, to guide and explain,
The difference between college and corporate terrain.

College CGPA sums up individual might,
Corporate CGPA sums up team performance, day and
night.
Total Revenue divided by employee count,
A formula that's new, a reality to mount.

If others falter, your growth is at stake,
A harsh truth, that young minds must undertake.
The 80/20 principle, a corporate creed,
20% drive growth, 80% reap the seed.

In college, 20% rise, 80% strive,
A different world, where talent survives.
CTC, a term, that's misunderstood,
Cost To Company, or Cost To Cut, as it should.

Companies aim, to cut the cost, to thrive,
A reality check, for young minds to survive.
Advice to young minds, as they navigate,
The corporate world, with its twists and fate.

Accept the system, with its flaws and might,
And learn to thrive, in the corporate light.